Winning Strategies for Admission to The University of California

Rachel A. Winston, Ph.D.
www.collegelizard.com
rwinston@uchicago.edu

Stand out. The UC application requires a strategy.

If you are uncertain about how you can gain admission, I will show you how to stand out and be accepted, even if you are not a perfect 4.0 student.

These pages invite you to discover how you can earn a spot at the University of California!!!

Why Trust Me?

I have walked thousands of students through the chaos and confusion of college admissions, from first-gen applicants unsure where to start, to high-achievers dreaming of top-tier UC and private schools.

As a professor, college advisor, and admissions coach with degrees from UCLA, Harvard, UChicago, Claremont, GWU, and more, I have helped students craft compelling applications and essays that go beyond grades and statistics.

I have also written and published more than forty books on college admission available on Amazon, including my recent best-selling 350-page book for high school students, *Medical School Bound*.

Whether it is cracking the code on UC personal insight questions or navigating waitlists, I have seen what works and built this guide to give you that exact edge.

ISBNs - Paperback 978-1-958558-56-0, E-book 978-1-958558-57-7

LCCN: 2025915931

We work with academic leaders who transform the educational landscape to publish relevant content and advise students of their educational and professional options, with the aim of developing 21st-century learners and leaders. We also work with students to publish their books and present widely diverse ideas to the college/graduate school-bound community. With headquarters in Irvine, California, Lizard Publishing works virtually with authors to edit, publish, and distribute both hard copy and digital books.

This book was published in the U.S.A. Lizard Publishing is a premium quality provider of educational reference, career guidance, and motivational publications/merchandise for global learners, educators, and stakeholders in education.

Book formatting by Obinna Chinemerem Ozuo (Ozuobinna@gmail.com)

Book website: www.collegelizard.com

About the Author

Dr. Rachel A. Winston is a tireless student advocate. She has served the educational community as a university professor, college advisor, statistician, researcher, author, cryptanalyst, motivational speaker, publishing executive, and lifelong student. As one of the leading experts in college counseling and an award-winning faculty member, Dr. Winston has spent her lifetime learning, teaching, mentoring, and coaching students. Her counseling practice centers around college admissions, college essays, portfolios, and intellectual conversations about life and career pursuits.

She started college at thirteen and graduated from college programs in such widely ranging disciplines as chemistry, mathematics, computers, liberal arts, international relations, negotiation, conflict resolution, peacebuilding, business administration, higher education leadership, interpreting, college counseling, and publishing. Throughout her education, she attended and graduated from Harvard, University of Chicago, University of Texas, GWU, UCLA, Syracuse, CSUF, CSUDH, Pepperdine, Claremont Graduate University, and Gallaudet University.

Her position working in Washington, D.C. on Capitol Hill and with the White House in the 1980s took her to approximately a hundred universities training campaign managers at colleges from Colorado to California, thoroughly dotting the western states. Later, she led college tours with students and their families on road trips throughout the United States. She has taught or counseled thousands of students over her career and speaks at conferences and academic programs throughout the world.

As a professor and avid writer for numerous publications, she won the 2012 McFarland Literary Achievement Award, Bletchley Park Cryptanalyst Award, and numerous other awards, including Faculty Member of the Year, Leadership Tomorrow Leader of the Year, and college service and leadership awards. While studying Human Capital at Claremont Graduate University, she was a scholarship recipient at the Drucker School of Management. She was also elected to the statewide Board of Governors for the Faculty Association for California Community Colleges, where she served on their executive committee.

She also served as a faculty member for the UCLA College Counselor Certificate Program and the Director of Mathematics at Brandman University. She taught at Embry Riddle Aeronautical University, Chapman University, Cal State Fullerton, and a handful of California Community Colleges, including Cerro Coso College where she represented the entire faculty as the Academic Senate President and retired in 2016. Over her career, she taught mathematics on television, in small and large lecture halls, online, and via live interactive satellite and telecourses.

Imagine seeing your UC acceptance letter. This guide will help make that moment real for you!

Testimonials

"I have officially chosen a school…UCLA!!!! I am beyond excited 😄 At first, I had gotten into every school but waitlisted at UCLA. Thankfully, after spending every day anxiously refreshing my email, I got off the waitlist. Rachel, you are the absolute best!" - Lauren B

"I remember how confusing the UC application was. I really wasn't sure if I was 'good enough' or if my grades were high enough. But I got in because of Dr. Winston, who miraculously brainstormed solutions on the spot." - Kendall K

"Getting into Berkeley is a dream come true. I honestly did not think I would get in, but when I received the letter, I screamed so loud you could have probably heard me in another country.

Thank you, Dr. Winston!"

- Brandon B

BUT, first for some Myth Busting….

"Yes, but… I need perfect grades."

To be crystal clear…the UCs care about more than stats. Your story, activities, and essay matter just as much.

"Yes, but…I'm just average."

Remember…what may seem to you to be "average" could actually be your unique edge. It is all about authentically presenting yourself.

"Yes, but…My extracurriculars aren't impressive."

It is not about how *many* you have. It is about how much of yourself you poured into the effort, whether or not you were a leader…and the *personal insights* you gleaned from your experience.

Table of Contents

Chapter 1:
Understanding the UC System

The uniqueness of the UC's mission, values, and structure of California's world-class public university system

I.   The UC System & Why It Matters

    A. Overview of the UC system's prestige and global reputation
    B. Role in shaping California's educational and economic landscape

The University of California system stands as one of the most prestigious and ambitious public university systems in the world. For nearly a hundred years, the UC schools were free. Today, the university charges tuition and fees for in-state students comparable to the top five flagship universities in the country.

With ten campuses scattered across the state, from the cutting-edge innovation of UC Berkeley and UCLA to the research-focused culture of UC San Diego and UC Davis, the UC system offers a powerful and dynamic higher education experience.

Campus	Founded	Location	Undergrad Enrollment	Graduate 2024-2025
UC Berkeley	1868	Berkeley (East Bay)	33,070	12,812
UC Davis	1905	Davis (Sacramento Area)	34,239	~7,000
UC Irvine	1965	Irvine (Orange County)	29,500	~7,000
UCLA	1919	Los Angeles	33,040	13,638
UC Merced	2005	Merced (Central Valley)	8,372	738
UC Riverside	1954	Riverside (Inland Empire)	22,646	3,780
UC San Diego	1960	La Jolla (San Diego area)	34,955	10,318
UC Santa Barbara	1944	Santa Barbara	23,232	2,836
UC Santa Cruz	1965	Santa Cruz (Central Coast)	17,940	1,998
UC San Francisco	1873	UCSF is exclusively graduate-level, specializing in medicine, pharmacy, dentistry, nursing, biomedical science, and public health		

For high school students and their families, understanding what makes the UC system unique is a strategic advantage in the admissions process.

The UC system educates around 300,000 students annually and is widely regarded for its academic excellence, groundbreaking research, and public mission. As a whole, the UCs have produced Nobel laureates, tech entrepreneurs, political leaders, and pioneers in public health. However, beyond prestige, the UC campuses are engines of social mobility and public service, shaping California's workforce and fueling its innovation economy. If you are applying to one or more UC campuses, you are not merely submitting an application to a school. You are applying to be part of an expansive vision for education, equity, and impact.

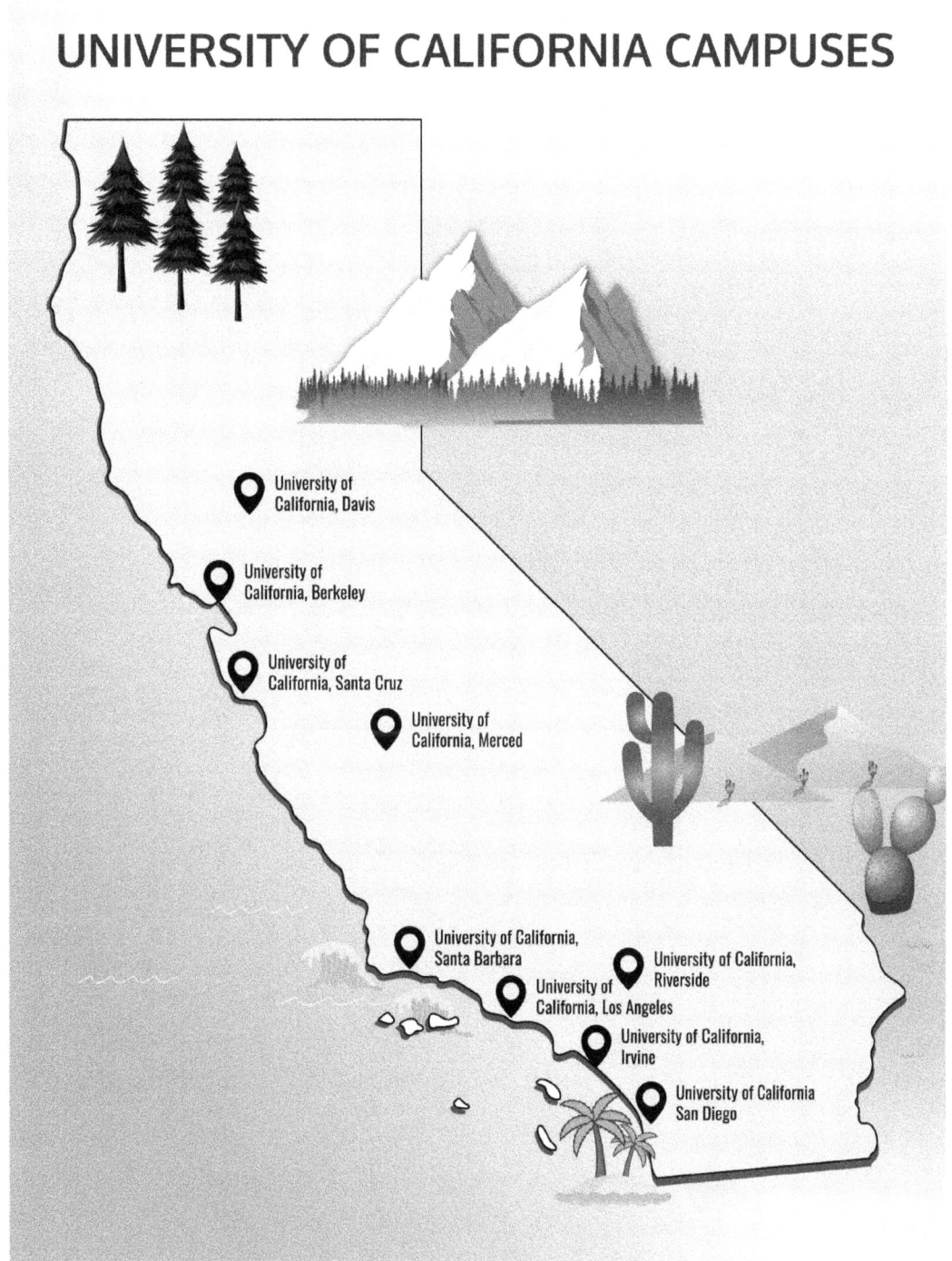

UNIVERSITY OF CALIFORNIA CAMPUSES

University of California, Davis

University of California, Berkeley

University of California, Santa Cruz

University of California, Merced

University of California, Santa Barbara

University of California, Los Angeles

University of California, Riverside

University of California, Irvine

University of California, San Diego

II. The Structure of the UC System

    A. The ten campuses: similarities and differences
    B. Governance: The UC Regents and the Office of the President
    C. Campus autonomy vs. system-wide coordination

The UC system is comprised of ten campuses: Berkeley, Davis, Irvine, Los Angeles, Merced, Riverside, San Diego, San Francisco (graduate/professional only), Santa Barbara, and Santa Cruz. While united under a single system, each campus has a distinct identity, academic strengths, and student culture.

The University of California is governed by the UC Board of Regents, a body that includes appointees from the governor, faculty representatives, student regents, and others. The system is overseen administratively by the Office of the President, which handles broad-scale policy and funding decisions. Even so, each campus enjoys a degree of autonomy, with its own admissions office, chancellor, and academic programs. This structure allows for both coordination across the system and the preservation of unique campus cultures.

III. Mission and Core Values

    A. The tripartite mission: teaching, research, and public service
    B. Commitment to access, equity, and affordability
    C. Diversity, inclusion, and social impact

The UC system operates on a foundational mission of *teaching, research, and public service*. This tripartite mission shapes every facet of UC admissions decision and education process:

- **Teaching**: The UCs are committed to delivering high-quality education that prepares students for civic engagement, leadership, and career success.
- **Research:** Each campus is driven by both faculty-initiated inquiry and student involvement in cutting-edge innovation across disciplines.
- **Public Service:** The UCs utilize resources and knowledge to enhance, improve, and serve communities both locally and globally.

At the heart of this mission is a commitment to *access, equity, and affordability*. The UC system remains one of the few elite institutions that offers high-level education while prioritizing need-based aid and socioeconomic diversity. Programs like the Blue and Gold Opportunity Plan ensure that eligible California students from **families earning under $80,000 annually can attend tuition-free**.

Diversity and inclusion are also woven into the UC's DNA. The system consistently leads initiatives to expand representation among first-generation students, underrepresented minorities, and students from underserved high schools. The University of California does not consider race in admissions due to Proposition 209, but it does evaluate a student's context carefully in student activities, essays, and other information provided in the application, including school environment, family income, and personal hardship.

IV. What Sets the UC System Apart

    A. The scale and scope of the research enterprise

    B. Access for California residents through the Master Plan

    C. The rejection of standardized testing and the emphasis on holistic review

Several defining features set the UC system apart from other public university systems:

- **Research**: The UC system brings in more than $6 billion in annual research funding. Students at every campus, including undergraduates, have access to world-class research facilities and opportunities.
- **The California Master Plan**: This framework defines system of community colleges, CSUs, and UCs, while ensuring that the top California high school graduates are guaranteed a spot in the UC system through pathways like ELC (Eligibility in the Local Context - top 9%).
- **Test-Free Admissions**: As of 2021, the UCs no longer consider SAT or ACT scores, although language proficiency tests are required for some students. This has transformed the admissions process, elevating the importance of GPA, course rigor, essays, and context.
- **Holistic Review**: Admissions officers assess applicants using 13 comprehensive factors, including academic achievement, leadership, creativity, and special talents. Each application is read in full, with no single factor determining admission.

These distinctive features mean that a student who understands the UC system's goals and philosophy is better equipped to tailor their application for success.

V. The Role of the A-G Requirements

    A. Ensuring academic preparation for all applicants

    B. Encouraging rigor and breadth across disciplines

    C. Impact on admissions evaluation

To be eligible for UC admission, students must complete the A-G course requirements with a grade of C or better:

- A: History/Social Science (2 years)
- B: English (4 years)
- C: Mathematics (3 years, 4 recommended)
- D: Laboratory Science (2 years, 3 recommended)
- E: Language Other Than English (2 years, 3 recommended)
- F: Visual and Performing Arts (1 year of a single art)
- G: College-Preparatory Elective (1 year)

These requirements are designed to ensure broad academic preparation. Health and PE are required, but do not count in the GPA calculation. The UC system emphasizes quality and rigor. Honors and AP/IB courses boost a student's GPA in the UC admissions formula, known as the capped weighted GPA. The cap is to ensure fairness since some schools offer few Honors and AP/IB courses.

Note: The UC weighted-capped GPA includes a maximum of 8 semesters of honors-level (weighted) courses for GPA calculation purposes (the equivalent of 4 year-long courses). However, students are highly encouraged to exceed the minimum requirements and pursue a challenging curriculum that reflects both their interests and academic ambitions, especially at UCLA, UCSD, and UC Berkeley.

VI. The Pathways to Admission

    A. Freshman, transfer, and dual enrollment options
    B. Transfer pathways and transfer guarantees with California community colleges
    C. The role of ELC (Eligibility in the Local Context)

The UC system offers multiple admission pathways:

- **Freshman Admission** is the most common route and applies to students coming directly from high school.
- **Transfer Admission** allows students from California community colleges to transfer into the UC system, often with junior standing. UC campuses reserve a significant portion of spots for transfer students.
- **TAG (Transfer Admission Guarantee)** provides guaranteed admission to six UC campuses for community college students who meet certain requirements.
- **ELC** identifies students in the top 9% of their high school class and offers them a guaranteed place in the UC system (though not necessarily their first-choice campus).

In all pathways, the emphasis remains on academic preparation, contextual achievement, and alignment with UC's mission, including access, equity, affordability, teaching, research, and public service.

VII. How Understanding the System Helps You Win

    A. Using insider knowledge to make informed application decisions
    B. Framing your narrative to match UC values

Gaining admission to the University of California is highly competitive. Most students and their families believe the process is mysterious. This book strives to dispel the mystery and some of the common myths. The more you understand about what drives the system and its admissions review process the more effectively you can position yourself as a strong match. Use this knowledge to plan your high school courses, build your extracurricular profile, and approach your essays with clarity.

When you frame your narrative to reflect a genuine alignment with the UC mission, you become more than just a qualified applicant. You become the kind of student the University system was built to serve.

Remember, the UC's foundational mission is *teaching, research, and public service*. Keep that in your mind as you present your love of learning, commitment to service, and desire to contribute meaningfully to research, innovation, and society. The following chapters will take you step-by-step through the most important elements of your application journey, from your course selection strategy to essay mastery. Understanding the system is your foundation.

> *"The university is not engaged in making ideas safe for students. It is engaged in making students safe for ideas."*
>
> **— Clark Kerr, author of the California Master Plan**

Chapter 2:
UC Admissions by the Numbers

Demystifying GPA, A-G, holistic review, and the 13-factor comprehensive review process

I.   Beyond the Numbers

   A. Understanding what data UC does and does not use
   B. Why GPA, coursework, and context matter most

When students and parents consider admission to the University of California, they often ask, "What GPA do I need to get accepted?" The answer is complicated because the admissions review process is holistic and there are many factors that enter into consideration. Frankly, GPA is only one of a set of criteria. For the University of California, who you will become transcends your GPA.

While GPA is undeniably important, UC admissions decisions are not based on numbers alone. Understanding how the UC system evaluates GPA, coursework, and the full context of a student's journey is critical to building a winning application strategy.

The UC system no longer uses SAT or ACT scores in its admissions decisions. This shift, which became permanent in 2021, places a greater emphasis on academic performance in the context of opportunity. The goal is not to reward privilege or perfection but to understand potential. The UC considers achievement, resilience, and commitment to growth. No single number can measure these factors alone.

II. GPA Decoded: How the UCs Calculate Your GPA

   A. Capped weighted GPA vs. unweighted and fully weighted GPAs
   B. Honors points: what counts and what does not
   C. GPA ranges at top UC campuses

UC calculates your GPA using a specific formula that differs from what you may see on your high school transcript. This is known as the capped weighted GPA. While this revised GPA is different than the one typically listed on your transcript, it is not mysterious.

The UC GPA includes:

   • 10th and 11th grade A-G courses
   • Courses taken in the summers after 9th, 10th, and 11th grades
   • Up to 8 semesters of honors points (One extra point for grades of C or higher in approved AP, IB, UC-Certified honors, or college courses)
   • A maximum of 2 honors points in 10th grade

In-state applicants benefit since schools have already approved UC honors and AP courses. Nevertheless, out-of-state students still earn honors points for AP/IB and transferable college courses.

There are three common GPA calculations:

1. **Unweighted GPA**: 4.0 scale with no extra points for honors or AP
2. **Weighted and uncapped GPA**: includes all honors points with no limit
3. **Capped weighted GPA**: includes honors points but caps them at 8 semesters

Most UC campuses publish GPA ranges for admitted freshmen, especially the capped weighted GPA. At UCLA and UC Berkeley, though, the middle 50% capped GPA ranges often exceed 4.20, while other campuses have slightly lower ranges. Still, within the competitive process, your goal is to complete the most challenging curriculum and earn the best grades you can.

III. Mastering the A-G Requirements

    A. Review of A-G subject areas

    B. Why exceeding the minimums matters

    C. The role of course rigor in admissions

To be eligible for the University of California, students must complete the A-G subject requirements with a minimum grade of C in each course:

- A: History/Social Science (2 years)
- B: English (4 years)
- C: Mathematics (3 years required, 4 recommended)
- D: Laboratory Science (2 years required, 3 recommended, 4 for STEM majors)
- E: Language Other Than English (2 years required, 3 recommended)
- F: Visual and Performing Arts (1 year in a single art)
- G: College-Preparatory Elective (1 year)

Students aiming for competitive UC campuses should exceed the minimums where possible and take the most rigorous options available, especially in highly competitive majors. UC values students who challenge themselves across disciplines and show intellectual curiosity.

IV. Holistic Review: The 13 Comprehensive Factors

    A. Overview of the holistic admissions process

    B. Deep dive into each of the 13 factors used by UCs

    C. Examples of how context influences evaluation

Every UC campus uses comprehensive review to evaluate applicants. This means that no one factor determines admission. Each application is read in full, and readers use 13 faculty-approved criteria to make decisions:

1. **Capped GPA in A-G Courses**

   Weighted/capped GPA in college-preparatory courses during 10th and 11th grade.

2. **Course Rigor and Strength of Senior Year Schedule**

   Strength of the 12th-grade schedule (APs, IBs, dual enrollment, college classes, etc.).

3. **Performance in A-G Courses in Context**

   Rigor and success in required subjects while noting school, community, and hardship

4. **Number of UC-Approved Honors, AP, IB, or College Courses**

   Focus on challenging coursework and academic enrichment while earning high grades

5. ***Special Projects/Programs in the Curriculum***

   Capstone Projects, AP Research/Seminar, Competitions, IB Diploma/Certificate, Magnet Programs (e.g. engineering, health, business, law, arts, medical, STEM, etc.)

6. **Academic Performance/Accomplishments Relative to Opportunities**

   Context: Review based on background, such as low-income, first-generation, or hardship.

7. ***Improvement Over Time***

   Notable upward grade trends, especially after difficulties in 9th or 10th grade.

8. **Participation in Educational Preparation Programs**

   Outreach programs like EAOP, MESA, Upward Bound, COSMOS, etc.

9. **Special Talents, Achievements, Service and Extracurricular Involvement**

   Commitment to the arts, school leadership, athletics, clubs, research, and volunteerism.

   Geographic Location of High School and Residence

   Consideration of opportunities available in the applicant's school and community.

10. **Geographic Location of High School and Residence**

    Overcoming hardship with resilience, persistence and creativity (wisdom from experience)

11. **Leadership, Motivation, Tenacity, and Insight**

    Demonstrated determination and commitment as shown in the Personal Insight Questions.

12. **Other Information Relevant to the Applicant's Academic Achievement**

    Work experience, responsibilities, or other context from PIQs or the application.

These criteria are designed to level the playing field. For example, a student who attends a high school with limited AP offerings but still takes the most rigorous classes available can be just as competitive as a student with a long AP transcript from a well-resourced school. Even so, many students applying to the top UCs go outside of their high school to take college classes so they are prepared to handle the challenges of UC academics.

V. Academic Breadth and Quality

    A. Course Selection: Pursuing balance and rigor in course selection across disciplines

    B. UC Honors Courses and AP/IB strategy

The University of California does not just want to see high grades. Admissions officers want to see students engage deeply with their education. Taking upper-level courses in math, science, languages, and humanities demonstrates academic breadth. Pursuing honors or college-level work shows ambition and preparation for college rigor.

Balance is also important. Do not overload on APs just to look impressive. UC readers want to know that your choices align with your academic interests and career goals. For students pursuing STEM, a strong math and science record is essential. For those interested in the arts or humanities, advanced coursework in English, history, or languages is essential.

VI. Special Considerations in the Review

    A. First-generation, ELC, low-income, or underserved schools

    B. Leadership, perseverance, and creative expression

    C. Handling grade anomalies or life challenges

UC readers are trained to consider the whole story of each applicant.

This includes:

- First-generation college status
- ELC status: being in the top 9% of your high school
- Low-income or underserved schools
- Unusual family responsibilities, medical challenges, or adversity

These factors do not guarantee admission, but they provide valuable context. Likewise, readers will notice upward trends in grades, perseverance in the face of hardship, and meaningful self-reflection in your essays.

Students who have strong academic ability but did not have access to APs or advanced electives can still shine. So can students who worked part-time jobs to support their families, or who demonstrated leadership in nontraditional ways.

VII. GPA Is a Single Piece, Not the Whole Puzzle

    A. How to build a competitive academic profile
    B. Using the 13 factors to guide your application strategy

UC admissions is competitive, but it is also driven by a humanistic framework. Although your GPA forms a strong foundation, it is not your whole story. A perfect GPA is not a requirement for success just as a few Bs is not a dealbreaker.

Instead, focus on what you can control:

- Take the most rigorous classes you can handle.
- Do your best in each course and seek help when needed.
- Use your essays to highlight strengths, growth, and character.
- Frame your experiences in terms of impact, learning, and resilience.

By understanding how UC evaluates applicants, you can make choices that reflect both your goals and UC's values. The next chapter will help you craft compelling essays that tie your academic story together with authenticity and purpose.

> *"Limitations live only in our minds. But if we use our imaginations, our possibilities become limitless."*

> **– Jamie Paolinetti**

Chapter 3:
Building a Standout UC Academic Profile

Course rigor, honors weighting, and A–G requirement strategies

I.   Academic Strategy as a Competitive Edge

   A. Why the right course choices matter more than ever

   B. Avoiding the GPA trap: depth over perfection

When it comes to impressing UC admissions officers, earning As is not enough. What matters more is the thought behind your course choices. You want to demonstrate evidence of growth, intellectual exploration, and the desire to challenge yourself. At the University of California, course rigor, consistency, and authentic academic interests speak volumes.

Many students believe that admission into a UC school requires loading their schedule with every possible AP class. However, you must work to your own level of ability or you will burn out. There is no perfect set of classes. You need to be thoughtful in your academic planning so your courses align with your goals, play to your strengths, and signal to UC readers that you are both prepared for and excited about college-level learning. Remember, the UCs look for potential. Show your growth and possibility.

Rather than chasing a high GPA, successful UC applicants often pursue a strategic mix of courses that reflect both academic ambition and personal growth. UC admissions officers do not expect you to outshine your classmates in every area. They expect you to be deliberate. There will always be someone better in one area or another. Do not fret.

UC admissions officers do not expect you to outshine your classmates. They expect you to be deliberate. There will always be someone better in one area or another. Do not fret.

II.   Choosing Classes That Impress UC Admissions

   A. Balancing rigor with realistic workload

   B. Which AP/IB classes carry the most weight

   C. When to take community college or dual enrollment classes

To stand out, you need to make wise course selections, especially in your junior and senior years. UC campuses reward students who demonstrate:

- A clear willingness to challenge themselves
- Consistency and upward trends in academic performance
- Choices that reflect future major or academic interests

Some classes carry more weight in demonstrating rigor. Suggestions for students pursuing these areas:

- **STEM:** Take AP Calculus, AP Biology, AP Chemistry, and AP Physics (if possible), especially for admission to universities such as UCLA, UCSD, and UC Berkeley.
- **Humanities:** Take AP Literature & Language, AP U.S. History, AP Government/Economics. For the top UCs, the IB Certificate or Diploma is desirable if offered or college classes outside if not.
- **Social Science or Pre-Law**: Courses in Economics, Psychology, Government, or college courses demonstrate continued interest in your area of study.

Community college and dual enrollment courses demonstrate rigor and commitment, particularly for courses your high school does not offer. Make sure they are transferable and align with A-G subject areas. These are doubly valuable when they transfer, eliminating UC required courses in your college curriculum. Some students save a semester or year of tuition by taking college courses in high school.

III. Maximizing A-G Rigor While Maintaining Sanity

    A. Planning a four-year academic, service, leadership roadmap that goes beyond the minimum

    B. Sample course plan ideas for STEM, humanities, and exploratory students

Course planning should begin early. Mapping out your four-year high school plan ensures you meet and ideally exceed A-G requirements. Here's a general framework:

STEM-oriented students:

- Math through AP Calculus by senior year
- Four or more years of laboratory science (some students double up)
- Strong foundation in English and history to demonstrate breadth

Humanities-oriented students:

- Four years of English, including AP/IB courses if available
- At least three years of history/social science (Consider taking extra community college classes.)
- World language to level 3 or higher (California residents should shoot for and earn the California Seal of Biliteracy to gain admission to the top schools.)

Exploratory students:

- Balance across all A-G areas
- Explore electives that spark interest or reveal strengths

You do not need to fit every category to the highest level. Just do what you do well.

IV. Understanding Honors Course Approval

    A. What counts as a UC-approved honors course
    B. In-state vs. out-of-state course recognition
    C. The importance of taking available opportunities

The UCs award weighted points only for specific types of courses:

- UC-certified AP/IB and Honors classes
- College courses that are transferable and approved

For out-of-state students, AP, IB, or approved college courses receive honors points; a few may not.

Students should take advantage of what is available. UC readers understand context and that some schools simply do not offer all courses. You will not be disadvantaged if your school offers few APs as long long as you take the rigorous classes offered.

V. Customizing Your Academic Path

    A. Demonstrating passion and consistency in academic interests; balance your curriculum
    B. Do not just take all STEM or humanities courses.
    C. When does it make sense to skip a year or switch a track

Admissions officers love seeing students pursue academic themes. For example:

- A student interested in biology might take AP Biology, Anatomy & Physiology, conduct research, and volunteer in a lab or hospital.
- A student passionate about political science might combine AP Government with Speech & Debate, Mock Trial, or Model United Nations.

You do not need to specialize too early, but consistency builds a strong academic identity.

Students sometimes wonder if they should drop a language or double up on math. The answer depends on your goals. The University of California appreciates both depth and balance, so make sure each decision is intentional. If needed, explain your choices in your application.

VI. Showcasing Intellectual Curiosity

    A. Pursuing academic opportunities outside of school; demonstrate interest in learning
    B. Self-study, online courses, academic competitions, and summer programs

Grades are just one way to show academic strength. You can go further by demonstrating genuine intellectual curiosity outside the classroom:

- **Summer Academic Programs** (COSMOS, UC SPARK, math, computer, or writing camps)
- **Academic Competitions** (Science Olympiad, History Day, MUN, Hackathons)
- **Online Coursework** (Coursera, edX, UC Scout, community college classes)
- **Research Projects or Writing Poetry, Books, or Newspaper Articles**

Highlight: UC Spark - Summer Program to Accelerate Regenerative Medicine Knowledge: an 8-week high school internship in stem cell research at UC Davis, UCSD, UC Riverside, etc.

These experiences can enhance your life experience and reflect key UC review factors, including special talents, motivation, and creativity. These can be showcased in your Personal Insight Questions.

VII. Excellence with Integrity

    A. Building a transcript that tells a compelling story
    B. Clarify your choices with context in your UC application

There is no single "perfect" transcript. However, there is a transcript that tells a clear and authentic story about you as a student. Choose your courses with intention. Strive for excellence, but not at the cost of your mental health. Challenge yourself where it counts. Then, reflect on how your academic choices reveal your curiosity, values, and future aspirations.

UC admissions officers seek to admit students who will excel academically and make meaningful intellectual contributions to the university. When your transcript, activities, and essays align to show that kind of student, you look strong on paper and present yourself as a future UC success story.

In the next chapter, you will dive into how to master the Personal Insight Questions. These 350-word essays allow you to bring your story to life in your own words.

"The beautiful thing about learning is that no one can take it away from you."

— **B.B. King**

Chapter 4:
Mastering the Personal Insight Questions

Crafting authentic, focused essays that highlight character, growth, and potential

I. The Power of Your Voice

    A. Why PIQs matter more than ever in a test-free admissions environment

    B. What the UCs are really looking for in your responses

If your academic profile opens the door, the University of California, the Personal Insight Questions invite you to step inside and introduce yourself. These four short essays provide UC admissions officers with the most direct insight into who you are beyond numbers. In a test-free world, your voice matters more than ever.

Each year, UC readers sift through tens of thousands of applications. What distinguishes one high-achieving student from another is often not GPA, but character. The PIQs are your best chance to convey that character. They showcase your resilience, curiosity, passion, and impact. The goal is not to impress with perfect prose or creative writing, but to connect through honest and meaningful reflection.

II. The PIQ Format and Expectations

    A. Four responses, each up to 350 words

    B. No ranking, no right answer, just insight

    C. Difference between UC PIQs and traditional college essays

UC applicants respond to four out of eight possible prompts. Each response is limited to 350 words. There is no ranking or preferred order. Every question is treated equally.

Unlike traditional college applications, which center on a single personal statement (often story centered), the PIQs are more focused and specific. Each one targets a distinct dimension of your experience or perspective. Collectively, they form a narrative mosaic that helps readers see you clearly.

The eight prompts cover topics such as leadership, overcoming challenges, creativity, academic interests, and community involvement. Choosing the right four is a strategic decision that reflects your self-awareness and ability to present a multifaceted identity.

III. Understanding the Eight Prompts

    A. Overview of each PIQ prompt and what it assesses

    B. How to choose the best four to highlight your life experiences

    C. Matching prompts to strengths, hardships, and challenges

Let's briefly review what each PIQ prompt asks:

1. **Leadership:** Times you took initiative or influenced others (A title is not necessary.)
2. **Creativity:** How you express originality inside or outside the classroom
3. **Greatest Talent or Skill:** A standout ability and its impact on yourself or others
4. **Educational Opportunity or Barrier:** Academic challenges or access to resources
5. **Significant Challenge:** How you overcame hardship and what wisdom you gained
6. **Academic Subject/Passion:** Your love for a subject, how it developed, what you learned
7. **Community Contribution:** Involvement, service, and impact that made a difference
8. **What Else?:** Open space for insights not captured elsewhere (family, circumstances, etc.)

Select four to six prompts that allow you to highlight distinct strengths. Choose your best four. Try not to overlap talents, situations, or experiences. Each response should offer a new and fresh perspective.

IV. Strategies for Strong Responses

    A. Focused storytelling with structure (STAR method)
    B. "Show, don't tell" is the operative mantra by harnessing the power of examples
    C. Clarity, tone, and authenticity in your writing

Strong PIQs tell a focused story with a clear beginning, middle, and end. Try using the STAR method:

- **S**ituation: Set the scene
- **T**ask: What was the challenge or goal?
- **A**ction: What did you do?
- **R**esult: What was the outcome or insight?

For example, instead of saying, "I showed leadership as club president," describe a moment of tension, a difficult decision, or an innovation you led. Use vivid language to pull the reader into your experience.

Also, make sure your response includes reflection. What did you learn? How did you grow? What will you carry forward? As you write, keep saying, "What is my PERSONAL INSIGHT?"

V. Avoiding Common Mistakes

    A. Clichés, vagueness, and repetition
    B. Repeating your resume or writing as if the essay is a job interview
    C. Ignoring the "insight" part of the PIQ.

Here are some missteps to avoid:

- **Being too vague**: General claims without examples fall flat. Avoid over-editing!
- **Writing a laundry list of your experiences**: Focus on one experience per PIQ.
- **Using big words to sound smart**: Clear, direct language is more powerful.
- **Skipping insight**: Without reflection, a story is just a story. Make it memorable.
  Repeat the word "insight" so you are clear about the focus. What insights did you glean?

Remember, UC readers are not just evaluating what you did; they are looking at the big picture of who you are, how you think, and who you are becoming. Consider how you showcase your potential.

VI. Real Examples and What Works

Here's an excerpt from a strong PIQ response on creativity:

"As the only student in my AP Chemistry class who spoke both English and Spanish fluently, I created illustrated guides for my classmates whose fluency was stronger in Spanish. One day, a student shared that my drawing of a molecule looked like a dragon. So, we named it, 'Dragón de Acidez', which became an inside class joke that led to naming other molecules as pneumonic devices."

Why this works:

- Specific example, rooted in context
- Demonstrates initiative, creativity, and empathy

Here's an excerpt from a strong PIQ response on overcoming adversity:
"At 15, I started scrubbing hospital floors at night to help my family stay afloat. By morning, I was back in class, exhausted but determined. When my physics teacher told me I did not belong in AP, I nodded, but stayed. I taught myself circuits using YouTube and built a mini wind turbine out of junkyard scraps. The night shifts never got easier, but the turbine still spins outside our window, humming with possibility."

Why it works:

- Emotionally grounded: The reader senses hardship, resilience, and resourcefulness without pity.
- Specific and visual: "Wind turbine out of junkyard scraps" creates a strong mental image.
- Growth arc: Demonstrate initiative and intellectual curiosity and ighlights grit and self-direction.

Here's an excerpt from a strong PIQ response on leadership:

"When my teammates lost interest in the robotics club, I did not step down, I looked for ways to improve. I rewrote our plan, trained two freshmen, and emailed local engineers for mentorship. By competition day, we were not just a team again, we won second place in design. However, my real win came when a student I had mentored said she was applying to engineering programs because of me."

Why it works:

- Leadership redefined: Focus on taking initiative, restoring morale, and empowering others.
- Concrete action: Shows specific steps, including planning, teaching, outreach without self-praise.
- Lasting impact: The goal is someone else's growth, sharing credit and emphasizing mentorship.

Your PIQs does not have to be dramatic. Everyday experiences, when told with insight, can be deeply powerful. Pretend you are telling an insightful story about backpacking, painting, or robotics.

VII. Final Tips and Review Process

    A. Leave time to draft and receive feedback without losing your voice
    B. Use the UC PIQ guide and review checklist

A great PIQ takes time. Here's how to approach your writing:

- **Start early**: Brainstorm ideas for each prompt and free-write.
- **Get feedback**: Ask a teacher or counselor to review, but avoid over-editing.
- **Read aloud**: Your voice should sound authentic and natural.
- **Utilize UC resources**: The UC Application Guide provides excellent sample responses and valuable tips.

Above all, stay true to yourself. Admissions readers want to know *you*.

The PIQs are not a test of who has the most awards or the biggest struggle. They are an opportunity to share four honest, human stories that reveal your values and your path. Embrace that opportunity.

In the next chapter, we will explore how to effectively present your extracurricular activities and leadership experiences. We will consider what you did and why it mattered.

Chapter 5:

Activities That Showcase Your Leadership, Impact, and Initiative

Framing your pursuits, talents, service, jobs, and passions

I.   Introduction: Why Activities Matter in UC Admissions

    A. The role of experiences in holistic review

    B. Moving beyond participation to personal growth

    C. Portfolios for Art, Music, Theatre, Dance, etc. (more in Chapter 12)

When it comes to gaining admission to the University of California, what you do outside the classroom matters almost as much as what you do inside. The UC system is deeply committed to holistic review, and one of the clearest reflections of your character and potential lies in your extracurricular activities.

Academic excellence may open the door, but your passions, commitments, and leadership show who you really are. Your activities communicate not only how you spend your time, but what drives you. Whether you lead a club, mentor peers, work part-time, or serve the community, your engagement outside of school helps admissions officers evaluate your initiative, values, and future contributions.

- You may list 20 activities, honors, jobs, and programs with a 350-character explanation
- Highlight your skills, creativity, passions, talent, leadership, and service
- Communicate who you are and where you commit your time, passion, and energy

Students applying in the arts will submit essays, videos, and images highlighting talent for some UCs.

II.   What the UCs Look for in Activities

    A. Impact, initiative, and sustained commitment

    B. Depth vs. breadth in extracurricular profiles

UC campuses evaluate your activities based on impact, initiative, and growth. They are less interested in seeing a long list of surface-level memberships and more impressed by experiences where you:

- Took initiative to start or improve something
- Made a measurable impact on a group or cause
- Showed sustained commitment over time
- Took on increasing responsibility

There is no "ideal" combination of activities. What matters most is that your choices are intentional and reflective of your interests.

III. Categories of Activities That Stand Out

    A. Leadership in clubs, sports, and student government

    B. Academic competitions and enrichment

    C. Community service and social advocacy

    D. Jobs, internships, and family responsibilities

    E. Creative pursuits and personal projects

Here are several categories of involvement that often stand out when thoughtfully presented:

- **Leadership roles** in student government, clubs, or organizations, especially when you led new initiatives or helped others succeed; leading clubs, sports, activities, and family
- **Academic enrichment**, such as math meets, Model United Nations, Mock Trial, research projects, coding camps, robotics competitions, or writing awards
- **Community service** that shows compassion, consistency, and a sense of social responsibility
- **Paid jobs or family obligations**, which demonstrate maturity, time management, and resilience
- **Creative pursuits** such as filmmaking, writing, music composition, or entrepreneurship

Every student's story is different. UC reviewers respect a wide range of engagements. What they want to see is authenticity, purpose, and growth.

IV. Framing Your Role and Contribution

    A. Using the STAR method to describe activities

    B. Highlighting initiative and problem-solving

    C. Showing growth, not just achievement

One of the most common mistakes in the Activities & Awards section is listing roles without describing impact. Instead of saying, "Member of Robotics Club," ask yourself:

- Did I take on a leadership role?
- Did I help my team solve a technical problem?
- Did I mentor younger members or organize events?
- What did we accomplish and why did it matter?

Use a **mini-STAR method** to describe what you did:

- **S/T**: What was your goal or role?
- **A**: What action did you take?
- **R**: What was the outcome or impact?

Keep it concise, but concrete. Show that you were not a passive participant, but an active contributor.

V. Using the UC Activities & Awards Section Strategically

A. Choosing the top 20 activities (better if put in order of importance)

B. Writing strong, concise descriptions

C. Prioritizing by impact and relevance

The UC application allows you to enter up to 20 activities or awards, spread across several categories:

- Coursework not captured elsewhere
- Educational prep programs (e.g., EAOP, COSMOS)
- Volunteer and community service
- Work experience
- Extracurricular activities
- Awards and honors

Each entry includes space for a description of up to 350 characters. For volunteer service, work experience, and awards, you get an extra 250 characters to describe the organization. The limited character count means every letter counts. Use action verbs. Focus on impact. Avoid repetition.

Example 1:

"As the club treasurer, I digitized our group's budgeting system to improve transparency and reduce waste. By tracking expenses in real-time and forecasting costs, I cut overspending by 25%. These savings funded our first schoolwide showcase, boosting club visibility and inspiring over 50 new members to join the following semester."

Example 2:

"To earn my Eagle Scout rank, I led a public service project at Canyon Crest Forest. I raised $2,000, coordinated with rangers, and organized a 12-person team to design and install 15 durable signs at each fork in the trail. Our work improved navigation and safety for over 300 monthly hikers and reduced search-and-rescue calls in the area."

Example 3:

"At Laguna Homeless Shelter, I served meals, restocked supplies, and listened to residents' stories with interest. I started a partnership with a local grocery store, boosting donated hygiene supplies by 30%. I also helped a resident craft his first resume in 5 years. His eyes glowed with excitement as we went online together in search of jobs."

Example 4:

"As co-captain of Tiger Advance, a competitive hip-hop dance team, I choreographed routines and led intensive practices with enthusiasm. When a teammate became injured before State, I changed our entire routine in 48 hours, setting up a revised practice schedule. Our adaptability paid off. Our talented team won 2nd place."

Example 5:

> "As the starting running back for Graham Tree High's varsity team, I trained daily to master plays, read defenses, and build trust with my quarterback. After tearing my hamstring junior year, I devoted months to recovery. My return and the cohesiveness of our team helped us win the league title. I rushed for 900+ yards and regained my momentum."

Prioritize your list. Put your most meaningful, impactful, or relevant activities first. Readers may not get through all 20, so frontload your strongest experiences.

VI. Aligning Activities with Your PIQs and Academic Story

    A. Creating thematic consistency across the application
    B. Avoiding redundancy while reinforcing strengths

Your activities and PIQs should work together but not duplicate each other. If you wrote a PIQ about organizing a voter registration drive, you do not need to repeat all the same details in the Activities section. Instead, summarize the effort and impact, and let the PIQ provide the personal insight.

Your activities can also reinforce your academic narrative.

For instance:

- A student interested in engineering might list CAD projects, robotics, and math tutoring
- A pre-med student might show hospital volunteering, first aid certification, and biology Olympiad

Consistency strengthens your application by helping readers envision how you will contribute your commitments on a UC campus.

VII. Building a Narrative of Meaningful Engagement

    A. Making your activities work together to tell a compelling story
    B. Demonstrating purpose, leadership, and potential

In a competitive applicant pool, activities offer a chance to distinguish yourself not just by what you did, but by how and why you pursued that activity. Leadership can manifest itself in various ways, such as organizing a food drive, designing a website for a nonprofit, or taking responsibility for your family. Passion can emerge from a part-time job at a bakery or an independent podcast about mental health.

Your goal is to present a cohesive picture of someone who is curious, capable, and committed to making an impact. Your activities should align with your values and ambitions. When you describe each with clarity and reflection, you will not just check a box, but you will leave a lasting impression.

Next, we will delve into how to create a strategic campus list that reflects your strengths, values, and goals across the University of California system.

Chapter 6:
Strategic UC Campus Selection

Analyzing campus culture, selectivity, and opportunities to create a balanced UC list

I.   The Myth of "Dream Schools"

   A. Shifting the focus from prestige to fit
   B. How to take ownership of your college list

When it comes to applying to the University of California, students often fixate on one or two "dream" schools, typically Berkeley or UCLA. But with nine undergraduate campuses, every UC has something exceptional to offer. The most successful applicants are those who do not just apply to the campuses everyone else wants. Wise students apply to the campuses where they are most likely to thrive.

While most students rise to the challenge of Berkeley's ultra-competitive academics out of fear, brute force, or to avoid embarrassment, many suffer from extreme anxiety. Competing on a grade curve with the top students in the country is not easy and may not be a good fit. Be careful what you wish for.

The concept of a dream school often leads students to narrow thinking. Instead, approach your UC list with inquisitiveness. What environment will challenge and support you? Which matches your values? Where will you thrive? Where can you get internships, research, study abroad, and new experiences?

Shifting your mindset from prestige to fit gives you control. Look deeper than the university's advertisements. Ask current students questions about opportunities rather than just parties. Look for those that offer help with internships, jobs, and graduate school admissions, rather than just social life. Be empowered to focus on finding the schools that will see your strengths and invest in your success.

II. Overview of the Ten UC Campuses (nine undergrad, one graduate)

A. Brief descriptions of each campus's strengths and atmosphere

B. Understanding undergraduate focus, location, and size

Each UC campus has its own identity and academic strengths. Here's a quick snapshot:

- **UC Berkeley**: Rigorous, politically active, and deeply research-oriented across disciplines, Berkeley is the top public research university. Renowned for its strength in engineering, computer science, and social sciences, UC Berkeley provides innovative programs like EECS and the Goldman School of Public Policy. The university also houses the top-ranked Haas School of Business and the Space Sciences Laboratory. You will work harder than you ever imagined.

- **UCLA**: This urban university is competitive and balanced in arts, athletics, and research. UCLA excels in the life sciences, film/television, and psychology, offering world-class programs through the David Geffen School of Medicine and the School of Theater, Film and Television. UCLA is also a leader in public health and biomedical research. Active, persistent, and driven students thrive.

- **UC San Diego**: This STEM powerhouse offers a residential system model and prime coastal location. UCSD is internationally recognized for oceanography, neuroscience, and bioengineering with the Scripps Institution of Oceanography and the Jacobs School of Engineering. The campus is also solid in cognitive science and machine learning. UCSD is known for its 8 living/learning areas.

- **UC Davis**: UCD's top programs include agriculture, environmental science, plant/animal biology, and viticulture. Its School of Veterinary Medicine is consistently ranked #1 in the U.S. UC Davis is a national leader in sustainability. UCD exudes its welcoming, relaxed, green, bike town culture.

- **UC Irvine**: This clean, suburban campus has growing programs in computer science, business, and health sciences. UCI is also known for innovative research in engineering, public health, artificial intelligence, and human-computer interaction. The School of Medicine and Program in Public Health emphasize health equity, biomedical innovation, and cutting-edge research.

- **UC Santa Barbara**: UCSB's laid-back, fun, outdoorsy beach setting offers popular programs in engineering, communication, and the arts. UCSB is strong in physics, materials science, and environmental studies with multiple Nobel laureates and the Kavli Institute for Theoretical Physics. Its College of Creative Studies encourages high-level research in STEM and the arts.

- **UC Santa Cruz**: Progressive and creative, UCSC offers top programs in astronomy, gaming, and social justice. UCSC stands out for astronomy, marine biology, and game design, with the Lick Observatory and a pioneering undergraduate game design major. It is also highly regarded for its interdisciplinary programs and social justice-oriented humanities research. The campus is filled with trees, serene walkways, and even deer. Many students take advantage of nearby internships.

- **UC Riverside**: UCR's highly diverse campus is dedicated to promoting social mobility and jobs. UCR's strengths include agricultural research, entomology, and creative writing, with its Citrus Research Center and nationally recognized MFA program. UCR is a hub for research in ethnic studies, criminal justice, and law, though medicine and healthy equity are rising areas of interest.

- **UC Merced**: As the newest campus, UC Merced is growing rapidly with tight student-faculty relationships, student support, and a sustainability focus. UC Merced focuses on environmental engineering and data science, with cutting-edge research in climate change and water resources. UC Merced supports interdisciplinary undergraduate research and ranks high in upward mobility. UC Merced also has a BS/MD program in conjunction with UCSF, the only one in California.

- **UC San Francisco**: As a graduate-only campus, UCSF is world-renowned for medicine, dentistry, pharmacy, and biomedical research. The university consistently ranks among the top medical schools and research institutions worldwide, particularly in the fields of cancer, neuroscience, and global health. Students are serious, disciplined, and research-focused.

III. Academic and Research Strengths by Campus

    A. Flagship programs, labs, and faculty excellence

    B. Matching majors to campus-specific opportunities

Not every major is equally strong at every UC. For example:

- **Computer Science**: UCLA, UC Berkeley, UC San Diego, UC Irvine
- **Engineering**: UC Berkeley, UC San Diego, UC Irvine, and others.
- **Environmental Science/Engineering:** UC Berkeley, UC Davis, UC Santa Cruz
- **Film and Media**: UCLA, UC Santa Cruz, UC Berkeley
- **Business**: UC Berkeley (Haas), UC Riverside, UC Irvine

Take the time to explore academic departments, undergraduate research opportunities, and facilities/ labs support those programs. Many UCs also offer honors programs, research scholarships, and first-year seminars.

IV. Campus Culture and Student Life

    A. Social dynamics, political climates, and diversity

    B. Urban vs. suburban vs. rural experiences

    C. Housing, clubs, traditions, and support services

Academic fit is only one part of the equation. Think about:

- **Size and setting**: Would you prefer a bustling city like UCLA and UC Berkeley, a more residential campus like UC Davis and UCSB, a suburban environment like UCI and UCSD, or a rural campus like UC Merced?
- **Social climate**: Do you seek political activism like UC Berkeley, athletic culture like UCLA, entrepreneurial energy like UC Berkeley or UCI, or artistic expression like UCSB or UCLA?
- **Community Support:** Do you seek access to cultural centers, wellness programs, religious organizations, or resources for first-generation students?

Talk to current students, attend virtual tours, and read the student newspapers. These insider perspectives often reveal more than brochures or rankings.

V. Admissions Selectivity and Strategy

    A. Acceptance rate data and GPA middle 50% ranges

    B. Creating a balanced list: reach, target, and likely

    C. How ELC and geographic diversity influence strategy

Admission to UC campuses is competitive, and selectivity varies significantly:

- **Highly selective**: UC Berkeley, UCLA, UCSD
- **Moderately selective**: UC Davis, UCI, UCSB
- **Less selective (but still strong)**: UCR, UC Merced, UCSC

Use acceptance rates, GPA ranges, and historical admit data to create a balanced list of reach, target, and safety schools.

California students may benefit from ELC candidacy, which guarantees admission to one of the UC campuses if they are in the top 9% of your high school class.

Note: The UCs value regional geographical diversity and may consider location for admission.

VI. Using UC Tools and Resources for Research

    A. UC admissions data dashboards

    B. Campus tours, virtual events, and admitted student profiles

    C. How to evaluate "fit" from out of state

UC offers several tools to help you make decisions:

- **UC Admissions Website**: Provides GPA ranges, majors, and campus overviews
- **UC Info Center**: Public dashboards with extensive admission and enrollment statistics
- **Campus Virtual Tours/Events**: Tours, student panels, and Q&As
- **College Scorecard and Niche**: Campus life reviews, outcomes, and rankings

Make a spreadsheet. Track application requirements, dates, and impressions. The more informed you are, the more empowered you will feel.

VII. Choosing Campuses That Will Choose You Back

    A. Letting go of rankings to embrace mission and match

    B. Building a thoughtful, strategic list with intention

The most competitive applicants understand that selectivity does not equate to superiority. Each UC campus is part of a shared mission to educate, uplift, and transform lives through public education.

Instead of asking, "Can I get in?" ask: "Where will I grow, lead, and thrive?"

When you build a UC list rooted in self-knowledge, curiosity, and strategy, you increase your odds of admission and ensure the university you attend recognizes and supports your potential.

University of California

The University of California Fact Sheet data below from UC Admissions, says, "Data are Subject to Change". Nonetheless, here is a comparison between admissions to the class of 2024 and admission to the classes of 2026 and 2028.

The increase in applications to the University of California is in large part due to changes in testing requirements. Policies, prices, and class sizes also allowed for more students to be admitted. For the class of 2028, the University of California received 250,436 applications, an increase of 1.5% from the previous year.

UNIVERSITY OF CALIFORNIA ADMISSIONS DATA				
University of California Campus	Residency of Applicants	Number of Undergraduate Applications		
		Class of 2024	Class of 2026	Class of 2028
Berkeley	California	50,223	72,417	72,129
	Out-of-State	20,659	32,580	29,755
	International	17,114	23,195	22,320
	Total	88,026	128,192	124,204
Davis	California	54,570	65,367	67,912
	Out-of-State	6,505	10,748	12,267
	International	15,798	18,610	18,655
	Total	76,873	94,725	98,834
Irvine	California	72,391	84,743	87,517
	Out-of-State	8,000	14,309	15,732
	International	17,525	20,113	19,412
	Total	97,916	119,165	122,661
Los Angeles	California	67,877	91,544	92,290
	Out-of-State	23,016	34,627	31,841
	International	17,944	23,608	22,119
	Total	108,837	149,779	146,250
Merced	California	22,244	22,516	23,691
	Out-of-State	598	1,319	1,539
	International	1,534	2,208	4,121
	Total	24,376	26,043	29,351
Riverside	California	43,151	46,456	48,633
	Out-of-State	1,473	2,492	2,753
	International	4,628	5,417	6,034
	Total	49,252	54,365	57,420
San Diego	California	66,350	84,326	88,392
	Out-of-State	14,364	23,778	24,169
	International	19,320	23,112	21,878
	Total	100,034	131,226	134,439
Santa Barbara	California	63,269	73,575	75,523
	Out-of-State	10,988	18,432	17,466
	International	16,690	18,984	17,247
	Total	90,947	110,991	110,236
Santa Cruz	California	43,893	53,051	57,503
	Out-of-State	3,897	6,878	7,691
	International	7,213	5,937	6,503
	Total	55,003	65,886	71,697

Chapter 7:

Timing & Planning - Your Roadmap to the UCs

Staying ahead with application mile markers and deadlines from 9th grade to submission

I.   The Value of Early Awareness

    A. Why UC planning is more successful when it begins before senior year

    B. Avoiding last-minute stress with strategic foresight

Many students underestimate the importance of early UC preparation. The key to a confident and competitive UC application is not cramming all of the work into October and November of your senior year. Plan early and build a solid foundation throughout high school. Smart timing turns stress into strategy. After all, if you have not participated in school, the fall of your senior year is a little late.

UC admissions is comprehensive. Its application process is unlike that of the Common App or private colleges. There are no letters of recommendation and no test scores. There is no single personal statement. Instead, the UC application relies on a structured, holistic evaluation that includes multiple essays. You are rewarded by starting early, preparing thoroughly, and engaging in self-reflection.

By becoming familiar with the timeline early, you give yourself the space to build your story organically. This reduces anxiety and ensures that you submit an application that truly represents who you are.

II. The Big Picture: UC Application Timeline

    A. Key dates: application window, submission deadline, PIQs, financial aid

    B. How to time letters of recommendation for scholarships, submit program applications, and send transcripts (if necessary)

Here are the critical UC dates:

- **August 1**: UC application system opens
- **October 1**: FAFSA and California Dream Act applications open
- **November 1–30**: UC application submission window
- **March 2**: Priority deadline for FAFSA and Cal Grant
- **Mid-March to Early April**: Admissions decisions released
- **May 1**: Statement of Intent to Register deadline

It is important to note that the University of California does not use letters of recommendation or SAT/ACT scores for admission. However, some scholarships or honors programs may require additional materials. Be sure to check campus-specific requirements.

III. Year-by-Year Roadmap (Grades 9–12)

A. 9th grade: Foundation-building, exploring interests, getting involved
B. 10th grade: Deepening academic rigor and taking an active role on campus
C. 11th grade: Leadership, GPA focus, summer programs, and PIQ prep
D. 12th grade: Final polish, application completion, portal checks, and follow-through

Here's a breakdown by year to stay on track:

9th Grade

- Focus on a strong start academically. Take honors courses if available.
- Explore clubs, sports, competitions, and/or volunteer activities.
- Review the A–G requirements; ensure course plan alignment.

10th Grade

- Take on more rigorous courses if available (honors, AP, or dual enrollment).
- Deepen involvement in extracurriculars that matter to you.
- Reflect on challenging/inspiring experiences for your future PIQs.
- UC GPA calculation begins. UC grades are included from the summer before 10th grade.

11th Grade

- This is the most important academic year. Grades count through the summer after 11th.
- Step into leadership roles or take initiative in your activities.
- Start brainstorming and journaling ideas for your PIQs.
- Visit UC campuses virtually or in person. Go to private schools too, especially those that count demonstrated interest in admission and also give high-dollar merit scholarships.

12th Grade

- **August–September**: Finalize your college list. The UC application opens August 1.
- **October:** Draft and revise PIQs, finalize activity descriptions.
- **November:** Review and submit your application by November 30, December 1 for fall 2026 applicants. Check yearly since system glitches force date changes, though Nov 30 is consistent.
- **December–April:** Monitor emails and portals; some campuses accept updates (e.g., new awards, fall grades, honors programs, scholarship forms, verification/validation requests, special program applications like Berkeley Haas business application or UC art supplement).

IV. Application Season Breakdown

    A. **August 1:** UC application opens; begin filling in personal and academic information.

    B. **September:** Work on activity descriptions; outline and draft PIQs.

    C. **October:** Get feedback on your PIQs and revise as necessary. Review your entire application for accuracy. Note: The "Additional Information" section is helpful to clarify anything.

    D. **November:** Review final edits and submit by the deadline. Note: The online application is very slow in late November! Start inputting information early or you may be really frustrated later.

    E. **December/February:** Create your portals and monitor them for opportunities/requests.

    F. **February/April:** Await decisions and send updates (if needed).

    G. **April/June:** Waitlist submission, updates, housing requests, and surprise admissions. Many students get accepted off the waitlists. Don't give up hope! However, do not get senioritis either. The UCs may request your grades at the end of the semester before deciding.

There is no benefit to submitting earlier during the application window. Just submit by the deadline, and ensure that your application is complete. Start planning early so you think of everything. However, do not have regrets about what you missed by submitting too early before your application is complete and you have "blessed" your application. Some students even take a picture of them pushing submit.

V. Financial Aid and Scholarship Planning

    A. FAFSA and California Dream Act deadlines

    B. UC Blue and Gold Opportunity Plan

    C. Campus-specific scholarship programs and timing

Financial planning is a crucial component of the UC admissions process.

- Submit the FAFSA or California Dream Act by March 2 to be considered for need-based aid.
- California residents with family income under $80,000 may qualify for free tuition and fees through the Blue and Gold Opportunity Plan as long as they qualify for financial aid. There is no additional application.
- Research campus-specific scholarships, which may require separate applications or have early deadlines.
- Use tools like the Net Price Calculator to estimate costs at each UC campus.

VI. Tools and Planning Strategies

    A. Creating a UC application calendar

    B. Using checklists, reminders, and document folders

    C. Seeking support from counselors, teachers, and mentors

Stay organized with these strategies:

- Create a UC application calendar with key dates and milestones.
- Use a cloud folder to store drafts, resumes, transcripts, and awards.
- Develop a PIQ journal to collect ideas and reflections.
- Check your email regularly for UC messages and confirmations.

Seek support from school counselors, trusted teachers, or mentors. Many students also benefit from peer workshops or college access programs such as College Match, EAOP, or AVID.

Here are columns and rows I use in the Google spreadsheets I make for my students.

COLLEGE OR UNIVERSITY	Due Date	EA, RD, REA	Major	Request Info Done	SAT/ACT Scores Sent?	Recs Assigned	Research Abstract or Arts Supplement	Honors Program
UC 1								
UC 2								
Private School/Public Out of State 1								
Private School/ Public Out of State 2								

Additional columns include:

Interviews or Auditions	Scholarships	FAFSA/CSS Profile & Submit Dates	Regional Rep	App Submit Date	Login URL, User Name/ PSWD	E-mails, Phone Calls w/ Admissions	Admit Decision Date	To Do List

VII. Timing as a Competitive Advantage

    A. How preparation creates confidence and clarity

    B. Staying organized while staying present in your high school experience

A thoughtful UC application is not something you should rush. The information you provide is the product of years of growth and months of planning. Starting early lets you approach each part with care, from your course selections to your final PIQ edits.

You undoubtedly dedicated much time and effort to academics, activities, service, and commitments. If you do not start early and stay organized, you are likely to overlook a crucial piece of your puzzle.

Organization leads to confidence. Confidence leads to clarity. When you manage your time intentionally, you meet deadlines and tell your story with power and purpose.

In the next chapter, we will explore how UC admissions officers actually evaluate your application inside the review room, giving you an insider's look at the decision-making process.

Chapter 8:

Inside the Review Room

A behind-the-scenes look at how UC campuses evaluate applicants

I.   De-Mystifying UC Review

    A. The human side of holistic review

    B. How UC campuses balance fairness and excellence

For many students, the biggest mystery in the UC application process is what actually happens after you hit "Submit." What does it mean that the University of California uses a "holistic review"? How are your PIQs, GPA, and activities evaluated and by whom? In this chapter, we pull back the curtain and show you exactly how your UC application is read, rated, and considered.

The UC system evaluates applications through a comprehensive review process designed to be both rigorous and fair. There is no formula, no magic number, and no single factor that determines your admission. You are considered individually based on your whole application. However, they do need to make a decision between you and other candidates, so whatever you submit is the representation of you they will consider. Plan, begin early, step back, and look at what your application says about you.

Each campus uses its own team of trained readers usually admissions officers, faculty, or counselors to read every application in full. The goal is to understand your achievements, context, and potential within the framework of the 13 approved criteria. Go back to Chapter 2 for greater detail on the 13 criteria.

II. The Comprehensive Review Process

    A. Why UC uses 13 factors?

    B. Who reads your application?

    C. How many times is your application read?

UC's 13-factor holistic review process allows campuses to consider a wide range of academic and personal qualities. The most important elements include:

- GPA in A–G courses
- Course Rigor & Senior-Year Course Selection
- Academic Performance in Context
- Personal Insight Questions
- Special Talents, Experiences, or Achievements
- Leadership and Initiative
- Challenges Overcome

Each UC campus has discretion in applying these criteria. Your application may be read by one or two readers who assign scores or write comments based on how well you meet campus-specific expectations.

III. The Role of Context in Evaluation

   A. Understanding school, community, and opportunity
   B. Comparing applicants fairly without test scores

One of the most important concepts in the UC review process is evaluating candidates in the context of their life experiences. Readers are trained to understand your accomplishments in light of:

- What your school offers (e.g., AP/IB and Honors courses, clubs, college access programs)
- Your family background, neighborhood, responsibilities, and access to opportunity

For example, a student who attends a school with no AP courses but earns top grades and leads a tutoring initiative will be seen as just as academically strong and possibly more resilient than a student from a well-resourced private school.

IV. Reading the Application Holistically

   A. How PIQs, activities, GPA, and rigor are weighed
   B. Strength of senior-year program
   C. Signs of motivation, maturity, and contribution

Every piece of your application contributes to the full picture:

- **GPA and Rigor**: Readers look for strong performance in challenging courses, especially in 10th and 11th grade.
- **PIQs**: These essays help readers understand your mindset, values, and growth.
- **Activities and Awards**: Your pursuits reveal leadership, initiative, and sustained effort.
- **Senior Year Program**: A rigorous 12th-grade schedule shows academic ambition. Are you "In it to win it?" Are you intentionally seeking to be more prepared for college or are you taking easier courses because you want a "chill" senior year? After all, took the required courses, why not drop Spanish and science? You competed in sports for 3 years, why not quit?

Readers often look for a coherent narrative: How does what you do in school, at home, and in your community reflect your goals and identity?

V. Campus-Specific Approaches to Review

   A. UC Berkeley and UCLA's faculty-driven read process
   B. UC Davis, UC Santa Cruz, and the use of contextual data
   C. Differences in weighting for programs or majors

Each UC campus applies comprehensive review slightly differently:

- **UC Berkeley and UCLA**: Known for their multi-reader, faculty-informed approach. Essays and rigor carry significant weight.
- **UC Davis and UC Santa Cruz**: Known for emphasizing context and upward academic trends.
- **UC San Diego**: Uses a college-based admissions structure with criteria tied to the campus mission.

Some majors are more selective than others. For example, computer science, engineering, and business programs at many UCs are highly competitive, and applicants are often evaluated within the context of their intended major. Course selection in these programs is critical since you must have the foundation to start running from day 1. For example, earning an A in engineering physics at Berkeley or UCLA would be next to impossible without taking AP Physics while in high school. Seriously! UC admissions officers are compassionate. They do not want you to fail, so putting you in a no-win situation is unfair.

VI. How Readers Flag and Recommend Applicants

    A. Reader scoring and commentary

    B. What elevates an application to committee review

    C. Handling borderline or high-potential applicants

Each application receives a summary evaluation:

- **Scores** or **ratings** based on strength of academics, personal insight, and context
- **Notes** summarizing achievements or concerns
- **Flags** for special talents, first-generation status, or overcoming hardship

Strong applications may be automatically recommended. Others may be referred to committee review, where a group of readers or faculty members deliberate on borderline cases, special circumstances, or highly competitive pools.

VII. Complete Your Application with the Reader in Mind

    A. Shaping your application to align with UC values

    B. Building clarity, depth, and coherence into your file

Understanding how UC reads applications should inform how you write yours. Here's what you can do:

- Build a clear, consistent story across your PIQs and activities.
- Use your essays to add depth to your transcript, but do not repeat information.
- Reflect on challenges, values, and aspirations, not just achievements.
- Select your courses, activities, and experiences with intention.

UC admissions is not about perfection, but rather potential. Your application should help readers see not just what you have done, but also what you will contribute to the school and the potential you have to be successful in the future.

Final Note: This is a competitive process, though. The University of California admissions officers will select approximately one person out of three on the average. At some high schools only one out of five will be admitted to any UC for whatever reason. That means only one will gain admission.

Will you be that person? Will the student with the highest GPA be accepted or one with a lower GPA, but a well thought out application? Surprisingly, some students who should have been shoe-ins do not gain admission. Why? Submitting a last minute application because you are busy with tennis, cross country, ASB, volunteer service, and school might put you at the bottom of the list, even if you have solid classes and grades.

For 2025-2026, here are some approximate numbers:

UC Campus	Applicants	Acceptance Rate
UCLA	145,058	9.4%
UC Berkeley	126,796	11.4%
UCSD	136, 728	28.4%
UCI	124,214	28.7%
UCSB	128,983	38.3%
UC Davis	120,131	44.6%
UC Santa Cruz	77,773	72.9%
UC Riverside	82,904	87.5%
UC Merced	51,745	97.7%

Now, for some interesting (again approximate) waitlist numbers for 2025-2026

UC Campus	# Waitlisted	Waitlist Admits	Waitlist Admit Rate
UC Berkeley	7,853	26	0.33%
UCLA	15,023	1,211	8%

In the next chapter, we will analyze real PIQ excerpts and explore how successful applicants use voice and structure to make lasting impressions.

Chapter 9:
Essays That Resonate

Successful voices, stories, and suggestions for winning personal statements

I.   The Impact of Storytelling

    A. Why certain essays stand out in UC admissions
    B. What successful PIQs have in common

Some essays linger in the minds of UC readers long after they have finished. These stories are typically not about winning awards or launching nonprofits. More often, they are about honesty, introspection, and clarity of voice. In this chapter, we explore what makes certain Personal Insight Questions rise above the rest and how you can craft your own memorable responses.

Great PIQs do not try to sound perfect. They sound *real*. They bring the reader into a moment, a conflict, or a realization. They are not afraid of nuance or vulnerability. They are often revealing and share an instance of transformation of mindset. And they always show a shift in perspective or self-awareness. Think "growth through adversity" or how you gained emotional/intellectual maturity.

Many students want to tell the same story about language barriers, making friends, and adjusting to a new city or country, experiences with sports or coaching, or their parents' divorce. More than half of all essays are on these three topics. First, consider a different topic or, if you are going to write on one of these, approach what you share in a unique light.

Additionally, many students attempt to stand out by writing in a unique format like a poem or, more bizarrely, an AI output with a series of one to two sentence paragraphs and no thesis statement, just a chopped up story. A recent student excitedly sent me her AI-written story, saying, "AI was so good."

Consider your creativity or the uniqueness generated by AI with words you would never use and the obvious syntax AI loves to generate. Sentence structure with AI is often abnormal. You are not allowed to use AI anyway to write your essays and your application could be outright rejected or at least flagged for verification. Have someone read your PIQs to see whether they think you wrote each one. If they don't think they are teenage or authentically you, I promise you the admissions officers will not either. Some sound like adults wrote them, and, of course, sometimes they do...sadly.

Be careful. Most stories get lost in the weeds while trying to be different. Either the reader cannot figure out what you wanted to say, or they stop reading before you get to the point you wanted to make.

Successful applicants use storytelling to highlight identity, agency, and resilience. They avoid generalizations and instead focus on scenes, choices, and feelings.

II. Characteristics of Compelling PIQs

Across hundreds of applications, the strongest essays tend to share these qualities:

- **Authenticity**: The voice sounds like the student, not like a thesaurus.
- **Vulnerability & Vivid Storytelling:** The poignant moment is clear to the reader.
- **Specificity**: The story includes real details, names, places, and actions.
- **Reflection**: The student explains what they learned and how they changed.
- **Structure**: The response has a clear flow, often with a problem, action, and insight.

Let's now look at four sample excerpts to illustrate these qualities in action.

III. Excerpt from PIQ #5: Overcoming a Challenge

- Excerpt and context
- What works and why
- How it shows grit and emotional insight

"When the Wi-Fi went out during my online calculus final, panic hit. I reset the router. Nothing. My mother, who does not speak English, paced behind me, equally anxious. I ran two blocks to our neighbor's house and finished the test in her dining room, seventeen minutes late. The final was graded pass/fail. After failing, I advocated for myself and politely asked for the chance to retake the final. Through this ordeal, I realized that my determination is a quality that lives within me and one I will bring to college."

Why It Works:

- Shows a real obstacle and an emotional response
- Evokes the home environment and family dynamic
- Ends with reflection rather than perfection

IV. Excerpt from PIQ #1: Leadership in Action

A. Excerpt and background
B. Balancing humility with initiative
C. Framing leadership without grandiosity

"When our school's recycling program abruptly stopped, most students did not seem to care. I emailed our principal, drafted a proposal, and got funding for new bins. However, without any incentive to act, they sat empty. Realizing I needed a new strategy, I led lunchtime contests, created posters, and turned recycling into a friendly competition. Participation jumped 85% in three months. My experience taught me that leadership is not about a title, but rather about persistent, creative, and student-centered engagement."

Why It Works:

- Describes a specific problem and action plan
- Quantifies impact clearly and concisely
- Offers a thoughtful takeaway on leadership

V. Excerpt from PIQ #6: Academic Curiosity

    A. Excerpt focused on the subject's passion

    B. Tying classroom learning to real-world action

    C. Showing a love of learning, not resume-building

"In AP Biology, I wondered how animals detect earthquakes. My teacher assigned a final project. I decided to consider the relationships between animal sensitivity and earth movement. I delved into seismology journals, spoke with a UC Davis geophysicist, and developed a prototype utilizing motion sensors and sound. I worked with one of the graduate students who was studying a similar topic. He spent time with me gathering data. While the prototype failed to tie animal sensitivity to earthquakes and instinctual reactions to ground vibrations the research process fascinated me, particularly asking questions to professors and graduate students on topics that do not have easy answers."

Why It Works:

- Connects a curiosity to real-world exploration
- Includes failure and personal growth
- Shows intellectual drive rather than just achievement

VI. Sample PIQ #2: Creative Expression

    A. Highlighting originality and risk-taking

    B. Demonstrating perspective and imagination

    C. Avoiding cliché in creative writing

"I choreograph dances in my kitchen. Flour becomes fog; my apron, a costume. As I smile, eager to begin, I press 'record', capturing video on my phone while moving gracefully between oven timers. For my final dance class project, I filmed a solo to 'Clair de Lune' kneading bread in rhythm with the melody, using snippets from my recent baked creations. Dance, for me, does not just happen on a stage. The flow and feeling of graceful movement allows me to find beauty in repetition, chaos, and joy."

Why It Works:

- Fresh, sensory-rich imagery
- Blends two passions (baking and dance) in an original way
- Reflects personality and insight

VII. Takeaways and Writing Lessons

A. Tools and tips for refining your voice
B. Common mistakes in otherwise strong drafts
C. Encouragement to be bold and honest

You do not need to win national awards or have a dramatic story. You just need to write with clarity, purpose, and truth. Here are a few strategies to help:

- **Brainstorm deeply**: Go beyond the obvious answers to each prompt.
- **Use your voice**: Write how you speak, not how you think you should sound.
- **Revise for clarity**: Make every sentence earn its place.
- **Get feedback**: But do not let others erase your tone or perspective.

Common Mistakes to Avoid:

- Writing what you think UC readers want to hear
- Repeating information already found in other parts of the application
- Making the essay too abstract, obtuse, or generic
- Forgetting to include insight or self-awareness

Your PIQs are not about perfection. They should represent your depth and humanity. The more you dig into what shaped you, what matters to you, and what you hope to bring to a UC campus, the more your essays will resonate.

In the final chapters, we will review common pitfalls and myths in the UC application process and how to avoid them with clarity and confidence.

"Words have a magical power. They can bring either the greatest happiness or deepest despair; they can transfer knowledge from teacher to student; words enable the orator to sway his audience and dictate its decisions. Words are capable of arousing the strongest emotions and prompting all actions."

– Sigmund Freud

Chapter 10:
Warning - AI, Authenticity, & Verification

The University of California's warning to applicants to use AI or provide inaccurate or false information

I. Introduction

In the age of artificial intelligence, college applicants face a new frontier. AI, essay-writing tools, and editing software offer powerful advantages, but they also raise ethical concerns. The University of California, like many other schools, has issued explicit warnings about the use of AI and the importance of authenticity in application materials. This chapter explores the University of California's policies and how students can avoid jeopardizing their applications.

II. UC's Official Policy on AI and Misrepresentation

According to the UC Application Guide:

> "Providing false or misleading information, including using AI-generated content or material written by others, may result in cancellation of your application, admission revocation, or disciplinary action."

UC's warning is direct and unambiguous. Whether through a ghostwriter, generative AI, or factual fabrication, submitting inauthentic materials is a violation of the university's Code of Conduct. Applicants must understand that any attempt to mislead, even with good intentions, undermines the admissions process.

III. What Counts as "False or Misleading"

Misrepresentation goes beyond academic dishonesty. It includes:

- **Falsifying Accomplishments:** Listing internships or awards not actually earned.
- **Inflating Roles:** Claiming to be "president" of a club when one was a general member.
- **Inaccurate Hours:** Logging exaggerated community service or work hours.
- **AI-Written Essays:** Submitting ChatGPT-generated essays is ethically wrong.

Anecdote: The admission of an Orange County high school senior was rescinded from a top UC after a club advisor reported that the student had misrepresented his leadership roles. During verification, the UC learned that the student was never the co-founder and president, roles he previously claimed.

IV. The Ethics of AI Use in College Applications

AI is not inherently unethical. However, misuse occurs when students let AI substitute for their writing.

Consider the difference:

- **Ethical Use:** "I used Grammarly and ChatGPT to help brainstorm word choices for my PIQ response. I rewrote the PIQ first and used AI as a personal thesaurus."
- **Unethical Use:** "I typed the PIQ prompt with my personal information into ChatGPT and submitted what AI generated. I then read and edited the result."

UC admissions officers read thousands of essays. They can recognize generic, over-polished content. An authentic story with imperfect grammar often reads stronger than an AI-generated masterpiece lacking soul. Besides, AI-generated essays read in an unnatural way, often using strangely placed words.

V. Real-World Implications & Enforcement

The UC system has tools to detect fraud:

- Plagiarism detection software (e.g., Turnitin or similar tools)
- Internal comparisons between writing samples and standardized test essays
- Manual review by admissions readers trained to spot AI-generated language patterns

Anecdote: In 2023, a Northern California applicant submitted essays with suspicious phrasing. A follow-up phone interview with pointed questions revealed that the student could not elaborate. Their admission was rescinded. **Note:** Some students cannot even define or describe the words they used in their essays.

VI. Verifying the Truth: The Application Audit Process

UC conducts random and cause-based audits:

- Contacting references listed in activity sections
- Requesting documentation for honors or research
- Interviewing students to verify written statements

This is why it helps to keep a log or folder with:

- Supervisor names and contact information (Start early since it is often much harder later.)
- Screenshots of awards, letters, or certificates (Sometimes these get misplaced; take pictures.)
- Project timelines and deliverables (What did you do? How? When? Where? With whom?)

Anecdote: A student applying to UC Davis included a robotics competition in their activities. During a verification audit, they were able to produce a photo of the competition, their name on the team roster, and a link to a press release validating their claims.

VII. Best Practices for Staying Ethical and Authentic

- **Document Everything:** Use a spreadsheet or journal.
- **Work Offline First:** Draft essays by hand or in a digital document.
- **Get Feedback Wisely:** Ask trusted mentors who know you, not strangers or anonymous editors.

- **Use AI Cautiously:** Not as a ghostwriter.

Reflection activity: Highlight three experiences in your Activities & Awards section. For each, ask yourself: Could I provide evidence or articulate the details if I were asked to have an interview?

VIII. Reflection Questions and Self-Audit

- Did I write this essay myself, using my voice and insights?
- Could I explain every activity or accomplishment listed?
- If asked to verify or explain something tomorrow, would I be prepared?

These are not just questions for admissions, but for personal integrity. Your story, told honestly, will always be more compelling than one told by AI.

IX. Conclusion

AI is a powerful, but it cannot substitute your voice, your truth, or your integrity. The University of California wants to admit real students with real stories, not perfect essays written by an algorithm. As technology advances, so will verification methods. But what remains timeless is authenticity.

Use the application as a mirror, not a mask. Who you are is good enough.

Chapter 11:
Avoiding Common Essay Pitfalls

Common mistakes in tone, structure, and storytelling - what UC readers do not want to see

I. Why Mistakes Matter

    A. The role of clarity and intention in competitive applications
    B. How small errors can weaken otherwise strong submissions

No application is perfect, but some are compelling, complete, and easier to read. The difference often comes down to avoiding preventable mistakes. In this chapter, we look at the most common pitfalls UC admissions officers encounter and how to avoid them to maximize your chances of admission.

In a highly competitive pool, even small missteps can significantly impact the tone of your application. A vague essay, an undeveloped activity description, or a lack of academic consistency does not automatically lead to rejection but it can cause a reader to lose confidence in your readiness.

By approaching your application with intention and precision, you allow your strengths to shine through clearly and cohesively. The goal is not to finish the application, but to do it right.

II. Misunderstanding Holistic Review

    A. Assuming GPA alone guarantees admission
    B. Ignoring context, narrative, and non-academic strengths

One of the most common misconceptions is that GPA is everything. While a strong academic record is essential, UC readers are trained to assess your whole story. Overemphasizing numbers while neglecting context, reflection, or personal growth can weaken your file.

Remember: UC review includes 13 comprehensive factors. Neglecting your PIQs, activities, or senioryear rigor is a missed opportunity to differentiate yourself. Many students will take the PIQs seriously, while doing a poor job on the activities section, believing the activity descriptions do not matter. Yet, it does. Your activities tie your story together.

III. Pitfalls in Personal Insight Questions

    A. Clichés and vague language
    B. Focusing on accomplishments without insight
    C. Over-editing or losing your voice

Many students stumble on the PIQs, even when they have solid experiences. Whether rushed or not showing growth and insight, they fail to communicate the impact effectively. Common issues include:

- **Clichéd Language**: They might say, "I learned the value of hard work," or "This taught me to never give up," "I want to make a difference in the world," without explanation.
- **No Insight**: Simply describing what happened, with no reflection on what it meant, leaves the reader to miss the significance of your experience or draw inaccurate conclusions.
- **Over-Editing**: With numerous revisions, especially adding the voice, ideas, or words of a parent, counselor, or friend, a student's voice can become generic or impersonal.
- **Using Artificial Intelligence:** This has recently become such a huge problem that the UCs have now established detection systems and warnings, threatening that they will no longer consider your application. Watch for these in your portal so you can follow up with verification. Failing to consider students because of AI use has never been more common.

Strong PIQs show vulnerability, specificity, and maturity. Avoid broad claims and instead focus on a few vivid moments that reveal your character.

IV. Activity Section Mistakes

    A. Underselling the impact or using generic descriptions

    B. Listing too many surface-level involvements

    C. Overlapping content with PIQs without adding value

Applicants often leave valuable points on the table is the Activities & Awards section. The University of California allows you to list up to 20 entries, but quality trumps quantity.

Common mistakes include:

- Using vague descriptors like "Helped with events" instead of "Led a three-person team to organize a schoolwide fundraiser"
- Listing shallow involvements instead of highlighting sustained contributions
- Duplicating PIQ content without adding a new angle or specificity

Tell a story with your activity list. Highlight leadership, initiative, meaningful impact and your takeaway.

V. Academic and Course Planning Errors

    A. Not meeting or exceeding A–G with rigor

    B. Avoiding challenging classes in your senior year

    C. Dropping senior year courses, or showing inconsistency

Your transcript speaks volumes. These common missteps can send the wrong message:

- **Not meeting A–G requirements**: Especially in math, science, or language.
- **Not understanding the art requirement:** Students may incorrectly take two different semester-length art courses rather than one for an entire year.
- **Taking an easier senior schedule**: Readers notice when students "coast" in 12th grade
- **Missing a core subject**: For example, skipping senior year math/science or taking Forensic Science or Sports Medicine rather than either AP Physics or college Physics when applying to majors like Biology or Engineering. Physics is tough in college without advanced Physics.
- **Dropping a senior year class:** When you drop an A-G class in your senior year, UC readers want to know why. They frown on dropping classes. Get help with your classes as soon as you notice a problem.

Challenge yourself appropriately, and use your application to explain any changes in course trajectory.

VI. Application Logistics and Red Flags

A. Submitting late or with technical errors
B. Inconsistencies between application sections
C. Leaving blank sections that could add context or value

Another area to watch is application review. These are mistakes are often overlooked but easy to avoid:

- Submitting late or rushing at the last minute
- Uploading the wrong draft of your PIQs (Sadly, this is very common and you cannot resubmit.)
- Leaving optional fields blank when they could add value (e.g., ELC status, additional comments)
- Typos, inconsistent information, or mismatched dates

Proofread every section. Ask someone you trust to review your entire application for flow and accuracy.

VII. Applying with Confidence and Precision

A. Reviewing your application like a UC reader
B. Turning awareness of pitfalls into a strategic advantage

UC readers want to admit students who are thoughtful, driven, and ready to contribute. By avoiding common pitfalls, you give them a clearer view of who you are and what you bring.

Before submitting your application, read it as if you were an admissions officer. Ask yourself:

- Does each section add something new?
- Is my voice authentic and consistent?
- Have I demonstrated growth, purpose, and potential?

If the answer is yes, you are ready to submit your application. You told your story with clarity, confidence, and care.

Here are a few things to remember as you go out to pursue your dreams.

- Work ethic is everything.
- Excellence is expected.
- Learn what you do not know on your own time.
- Come to work prepared.
- Take constructive criticism well.
- Be respectful and courteous.
- Keep your cool under pressure.
- Avoid being timid.
- Stay on task.
- Come early.
- Stay late.
- Take your work seriously.

- Do more than expected.
- Be thoughtful and respectful.
- Read your e-mail/texts after hours in case something is important.
- Ask questions. No question is too stupid.
- Maintain a clean workspace.
- Dress and act professionally.
- Don't gossip or complain.
- Play when you are done.
- Avoid frustrating your phenomenally busy supervisor.
- Be straightforward, and don't beat around the bush.

You've Got This!

With that, your application has come full circle. From understanding the UC system to mastering the final polish of your application, you now hold the tools and strategies to approach this process with purpose. You only have one more step. Now, you just need to follow up with portals and communication.

Chapter 12:
Portals, Communication, and Art Portfolios

Connecting to each UC campus with a unique login and following up with missing/requested information

When you submit your UC application, the hard part seems to be over. Sorry. You have a few more steps. After submission, the next phase involves actively engaging with each UC campus through their own applicant portals.

Although you sent a single application, that file was sent to a central processing center. Now, you have to connect separately to each campus and then monitor and manage each communication channel individually. Staying organized, responsive, and informed during this period can significantly impact your admissions outcome.

I. Understanding the UC Portal System

The UC application platform is unified. You submit one application, pay fees (or secure fee waivers), and list multiple campuses. However, once the application is sent off, you are not directly connected to any of the colleges' admissions offices. In effect, you just sent the application to a central data bank.

Within a few weeks, you will receive a series of e-mails. One will arrive from each UC to which you applied, inviting you to set up their unique campus portal so you can connect directly. These portals serve as the admissions departments' post-submission activities, including document uploads, application status, verification, program applications, scholarships, financial aid, and official communication.

Each UC has its own timeline, portal name, and log in. Yes. They are all different. This can be confusing and time-consuming if you are not paying close attention. For instance, UC Berkeley uses MAP@ Berkeley, UC Irvine uses MyAdmissions, and UC Santa Cruz has MyUCSC. While these portals serve similar functions, they do not look alike, and they do not notify you in the same way. Some updates are posted frequently (via e-mail and/or in the portal), while others remain static until a decision is made.

It is important to remember that *no news is not necessarily good or bad news*. Some UCs are faster in reviewing applications or requesting additional materials, while others take longer. The key is consistency. You must log in regularly and make portal checks a habit to get updates. Most of the time, there will be no new information until, one day, a request arrives.

II. When and How to Access Portals

Typically, you will receive your first portal invitation e-mail from a UC campus within 2–4 weeks of submitting your application. The e-mails will come with specific instructions and a temporary login link.

Since the messages are system-generated, they may end up in your spam folder. Therefore, you must check your spam folder regularly. Remember, your computer will not recognize the address.

You will be asked to create an account or verify your identity with your UC Application ID or e-mail. Once you enter, save each of your login credentials on a spreadsheet. You will check frequently between January and March, and then again after decisions are released to submit statements of intent to register (SIR), housing deposits, or financial aid documents. You might need to request to be on the waitlist or write a statement of continued interest, fondly called a "love letter".

III. What to Expect Inside the Portals

Each UC portal contains slightly different features, but you can expect key similarities:

- **Application Status:** Whether your application has been received, is under review, or has had a decision posted.
- **Checklist of Required Items:** Some UCs require additional forms, verification documents, or clarification of self-reported grades. The portal will tell you if you are missing anything.
- **Financial Aid Tracking:** Once you have submitted your FAFSA or California Dream Act Application, you can confirm whether the campus has received it. Some campuses also allow you to upload documents, such as tax returns or citizenship verification, directly in the portal.
- **Communications Center:** This may include messages from the admissions office, instructions for missing documents, or invitations to interviews or events.
- **Decision Notification:** Most UCs will post admission decisions on the portal before sending out e-mail. This is why it is essential to check the portal, even if you have not received an e-mail notification yet.

IV. Campus-by-Campus Portal Guide - Quick Summary

- **UC Berkeley – MAP@Berkeley (My Application Portal)**
  Tracks application status, financial aid, and checklists; decision release first appears here.
- **UCLA – UCLA Application Portal**
  Offers a status update and financial aid information; decision date is posted early.
- **UC San Diego – Applicant Portal**
  Clearly organized dashboard; includes a checklist and "My Triton Checklist" features.
- **UC Santa Barbara – UCSB Applicant Portal**
  Posts decision early; financial aid tracker included.
- **UC Irvine** – Log in using your **UCInetID**, which you activate after submitting your UC Application. One of the more interactive portals with status tracking and document upload.
- **UC Davis – MyAdmissions**
  Similar in functionality to UCI's portal; includes a residency questionnaire and financial forms.

- **UC Santa Cruz – MyUCSC**

  Offers a detailed To-Do List and Message Center; also used for course planning later.

- **UC Riverside – MyUCR**

  Easy to navigate, tracks all materials and admission decisions.

- **UC Merced – Connect Platform**

  Newer design; integrates decision release and registration details.

Each of these systems is entirely separate, which means that uploading a transcript to UC Santa Cruz does not fulfill a request from UC Irvine. Never assume that information submitted to one UC carries over to another. It doesn't.

V. Following Up with Missing or Requested Information

You may be asked to clarify or update some of your application materials. Common requests include:

- Verification of residency/citizenship status or substantiation of activities/essays
- Corrected or updated coursework and grades
- Test score validation (if you included scores, like TOEFL/IELTS, in your application)
- Family income documentation for financial aid

Deadlines for these requests are non-negotiable. Failure to upload the correct document or missing a deadline may result in your application being withdrawn from consideration. Some requests will be emailed; others may only appear in your portal, which is why checking frequently is crucial.

When uploading documents, double-check file types and size restrictions. PDF is usually preferred. Always save a copy of your confirmation screen or email, just in case something gets lost in transmission.

VI. Who to Contact and How to Reach Them

If you have questions about missing materials or unclear instructions, use the contact information provided within the portal. Each UC campus has its own admissions office with its own staff. E-mail is typically preferred. Don't be surprised. Getting through by phone may be hard during peak times.

Here are a few best practices:

- Use your application ID in all correspondence.
- Write from the same e-mail address you used on your UC application.
- Be polite and professional. Every communication is a first impression on those reviewing your file. Kindness goes a long way, even especially when you are upset.
- Do not e-mail multiple campuses with a general question; target each inquiry to the specific admissions office.

VII. Communication Best Practices

Stay on top of your UC portals and communication. Demonstrate the kind of responsibility expected of college students. Here are some key habits:

- **Check your e-mail daily** and your UC portals once per week.
- **Create a spreadsheet** listing each UC campus, the date you received portal access, your login information, and any missing documents.
- **Respond quickly** to all requests or notices. Even if you do not have the requested item yet, acknowledge the message.
- **Keep all confirmation e-mails** and documents organized in physical and digital folders.
- **Avoid over-communicating**. Do not e-mails about responses already answered in FAQs or visible in your portal. Respect the staff's time.

If you are waitlisted, you must opt in through your portal to remain under consideration. In some cases, you need to upload additional statements or letters of continued interest.

VIII. Special Notes for International, Transfer, and ELC Students

If you are an international student, you may be asked for additional documentation such as:

- Proof of English language proficiency (e.g., TOEFL/IELTS)
- Copy of your passport
- Financial certification statements

Transfer students may have different checklist items, such as:

- Updates on planned coursework or grades in progress
- Transfer Academic Update submission confirmation
- Verification of Associate Degree for Transfer status, if applicable

California residents who qualify under the Eligibility in the Local Context may also have to confirm or update their high school information. Portals will direct these students accordingly.

IX. The Bigger Picture: Communication Reflects Commitment

One of the most underestimated components of the college application process is communication. The e-mails you send, the portals you monitor, and the materials you upload all form part of your admissions file. Admissions officers do not just assess your grades and essays; they note how you respond when something is missing or incorrect. Do you reply quickly? Do you follow instructions carefully? Are you respectful?

This is particularly important if you are navigating waitlists or appeals. Demonstrating reliability and interest through your follow-up communication can subtly, but powerfully, impress a campus. Remember, your portal is your virtual presence on campus before you are even admitted.

X. Submitting a SlideRoom Portfolio for the University of California

Several UC arts programs (visual art, design, theatre, music, and dance) require or strongly recommend a supplemental portfolio in addition to the standard UC Application. This supplemental material is submitted online via SlideRoom, a secure platform that allows applicants to upload media, documents, and responses to program-specific questions.

Step 1 – Apply as an Arts Major to the UCs First

You must list the arts major as your first-choice major. Shortly after submission, eligible applicants receive an e-mail with a link to the campus's SlideRoom portal for that specific program.

Step 2 – Access the Campus Portal

Each campus has its own SlideRoom link and requirements. For example:

- **UCLA**: Dance, Theater, Design Media Arts, and Music programs
- **UC Irvine**: Claire Trevor School of the Arts disciplines
- **UC San Diego**: Visual Arts, Dance, Theatre
- **UC Santa Barbara**: Dance, Theatre (in-person/video auditions)

Step 3 – Prepare/Upload Your Materials (Varies by UC)

- **Images** (JPEG, PNG, PDF for artwork)
- **Video** (MP4 or MOV for performances and dance auditions)
- **Audio** (MP3 or WAV for music performances or compositions)
- **Documents** (resumes, artist statements, essays)

Each program specifies what is required. For example, dance applicants might upload a movement video, choreography video, and personal artistic statement, while visual art applicants might provide 10–20 high-quality images with descriptions.

Step 4 – Follow Technical and Artistic Guidelines

Every discipline publishes its own technical specs (file size, time limits) and artistic prompts (e.g., "Submit two contrasting monologues" for theatre or "Provide two original compositions" for music). Read carefully; failure to follow instructions can disqualify your submission.

Step 5 – Submit by the Deadline

Most UC arts portfolios are due early to mid-December. SlideRoom submissions require a small nonrefundable fee, around $10–$20), paid online. Once submitted, log back in to confirm files uploaded correctly.

Step 6 – Review and Evaluation

Faculty members review portfolios holistically, considering artistic skill, originality, and potential for growth, alongside your academic record.

XI. Conclusion

Managing multiple applicant portals may not feel as exciting as writing your personal insight questions or receiving your first acceptance, but it is every bit as critical. Think of this phase as a test in time management, maturity, and diligence. These are the skills you will need in college.

To summarize:

- Each UC campus will provide its own applicant portal after submission.
- These portals are essential for checking application status, responding to document requests, and tracking financial aid.
- Deadlines matter. Communication matters even more.
- By managing your portals with care, you not only protect your application, you show that you are ready for the independence and responsibility of college life.

Your UC application journey does not end with the click of the "Submit" button. In many ways, submission is just beginning.

"Life is a matter of choices, and every choice you make makes you."

- John C. Maxwell

Chapter 13:

Personal UC Workbook

Your Winning Strategy to Gain Admission into the University of California

Apply the lessons from each chapter to plan and personalize your goal-setting. Complete each part step by step while reflecting on your life journey.

Section 1: Understanding the UC System

List three aspects of the UC mission that resonate with you:

1. _____
2. _____
3. _____

How does the tripartite mission (teaching, research, public service) align with your goals?

_____

Which UC campuses are you most curious about, and why?

_____

_____

Section 2: GPA, A–G, and Holistic Review

Enter your UC GPA: _____

How many UC-approved honors/AP courses have you taken?_____

What are your academic strengths and areas for growth?

_____

_____

Which of the 13 UC factors do you feel strongest? Circle three: [ ] GPA [ ] Rigor [ ] Context [ ] Talent [ ] Service [ ] Leadership [ ] Growth [ ] Resilience [ ] Academic Curiosity

When have you demonstrated resilience? _____

_____

_____

Section 3: Academic Profile Planning

Create your 4-year high school course plan or audit your completed plan.

9th:_____

10th_____

11th_____

12th_____

Where might you add rigor next year? _____

Section 4: Brainstorming Your PIQs

Write possible topics to each of the 8 prompts. Which feel most natural for you?

1. Leadership Experience

Describe an example of your leadership experience in which you have positively influenced others, helped resolve disputes, or contributed to group efforts over time.

_____

2. Creative Expression

Every person has a creative side, and it can be expressed in many ways: problem solving, original and innovative thinking, and artistically, to name a few. Describe how you express your creative side.

_____

3. Greatest Talent or Skill

What would you say is your greatest talent or skill? How have you developed and demonstrated that talent over time?

_____

4. Educational Opportunity or Barrier Overcome

Describe how you have taken advantage of a significant educational opportunity or worked to overcome an educational barrier you have faced.

_____

5. Significant Challenge

Describe the most significant challenge you have faced and the steps you have taken to overcome this challenge. How has this challenge affected your academic achievement?

_____

6. Academic Subject Passion

Think about an academic subject that inspires you. Describe how you've furthered this interest inside and/or outside the classroom.

_____

7. School/Community Contribution

What have you done to make your school or your community a better place?

_____

8. What Makes You Stand Out?

Beyond what has already been shared in your application, what do you believe makes you a strong candidate for admissions to the University of California?

_____

Note: In my experience, students who draft six are surprised to find that the extra effort required to draft the two they were not considering makes those essays much more appealing than the ones that they initially thought would come naturally.

Example: The PIQ on the big award you won may come off as pretentious or off-putting, whereas the elementary school where you taught sign language and inspired children might appear humbling.

Section 5: Activities & Impact Inventory

List as many as you have. The UCs give you 20 spaces, but you do not need to use all of them.

1. _____	11. _____
2. _____	12. _____
3. _____	13. _____
4. _____	14. _____
5. _____	15. _____
6. _____	16. _____
7. _____	17. _____
8. _____	18. _____
9. _____	19. _____
10. _____	20. _____

STAR method:

- **S**ituation: Set the scene
- **T**ask: What was the challenge or goal?
- **A**ction: What did you do specifically?
- **R**esult: What was the outcome or insight?

Research each UC and their majors. Which majors fit your interests? Have you complete the requirements of the typical candidate at that school?

Section 6: UC Campus Major Worksheet

UC Campus	First Choice Major	Alternate Major
UC Berkeley		
UC Davis		
UC Irvine		
UCLA		
UC Merced		
UC Riverside		
UC Santa Barbara		
UC Santa Cruz		
UCSD		

Section 7: Application Timeline Planning (the application opens August 1)

Check when done.

Start UC Application _____ Select Colleges: _____ Activity Statements _____

Finalize PIQs _____ Submit FAFSA or CA Dream Act _____

Submit UC Application (There is no benefit to early submission): _____

List three tasks to complete each month from August to November.

August _____

September _____

October _____

November _____

In early December, set up portals for each school (create a spreadsheet or Google Sheet)

December Portal Set Up_____   Winter Break - Portal Check _____

January - Check portals at least two times _____

Section 8: Reader Simulation Checklist

- Pretend you are an admissions officer. Review your application for:
  - o Clear narrative
  - o Consistency of voice

- Evidence of growth, service, or impact

☐ Write a 3-sentence summary of yourself as a UC applicant.

_____

_____

_____

Section 9: Final Reflection

- What is your biggest strength as an applicant?
- What part of the application are you most proud of?
- What UC value (access, research, public service) do you most connect with, and how will you carry it forward?

_____

_____

_____

Lizard Publishing creates, designs, produces, and distributes books and resources to provide academic, admissions, and career information. Our mental process is fueled by three tenets:

- Ignite the hunger to learn and the passion to make a difference
- Illuminate the expanse of knowledge by sharing cutting-edge thinking
- Innovate to create a world that makes the transition from dreams to reality

We work with academic leaders who transform the educational landscape to publish relevant content and advise students of their educational and professional options, with the aim of developing 21st-century learners and leaders. We also work with students to publish their books and present widely diverse ideas to the college/graduate school-bound community. With headquarters in Irvine, California, Lizard Publishing works virtually with authors to edit, publish, and distribute both hard copy and paperback books.

Below are a few of our books that you might find extremely valuable.

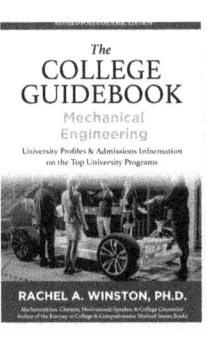
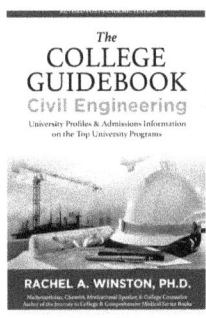
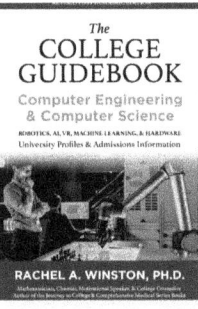

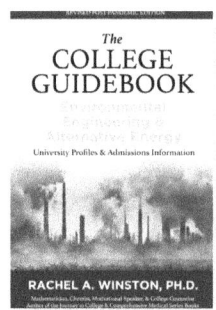

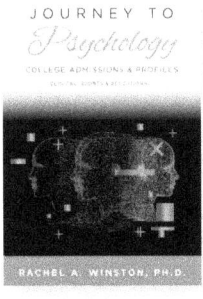

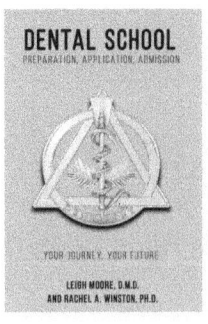
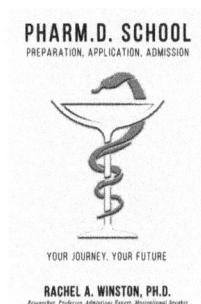